GW00854540

Reflections

To
Roz
with much love

John E Bruce

03/03/2011

Reflections

John Prince

First Published by *Baas Press* 2010

Copyright © John E. Prince, 2010

ISBN 978-0-9566961-0-6

All rights reserved. No part of this publication may be reproduced or transmitted, in any form or by any means, without written permission of the publisher.

Cover design by Arnold Prince

Copyright of cover design © John E. Prince

Prepared and printed by:
York Publishing Services Ltd
64 Hallfield Road
Layerthorpe
York YO31 7ZQ
Tel: 01904 431213

Website: www.yps-publishing.co.uk

CONTENTS

ACKNOWLEDGEMENTS

I acknowledge with deep gratitude, the love and continuous support of my dear wife Maudlyn, and my dear children: John-Eugene, Lesley, and Gerald. Their repeated prodding and words of belief, helped in no small measure, to the publication of this work.

My sister Althea has been my literary mentor and more than anyone, helped in making me focused, on the creative nature of my being and to share my experiences and perceptions.

I must thank my brother Arnold, for his support and for his drawing, which forms the cover illustration of this book and also my nephew Baden Junior, for his editing of some of my work.

Finally I acknowledge the literary example set by my father, Gerald Simon Prince and my mother, Dorothy Sebastian Prince, both of whom wrote their biographies.

RESTLESS SPIRIT

She reclined in comfort on her bed,
Relieved of daily toil
And stress, that she had shed.
She had sought not foil,
Throughout life's stride,
From these twin burdens,
Since she glowed with pride,
At her sacrifices,
For her home made tribe.
But now, relief had come through time,
As stealthily, age chimed
Its relentless toll
And stole
Her into feebleness;
But not of mind.
Her spirit was alert
And relished her noble history.
She did not mourn the past;
But gloried in her victory;
For in surviving, she had won.
She was my mother;
Steeped in years of tears and victories
Over obstacles galore;
For we were poor.
Many were the stories she would tell,
Of wasted lives in living hell,
Which she had shared.

Now, as her chronicler,
I clasp her as a woman;
And in her past, I dared
To peer, probe and disrobe
The outer garments,
Of the characters that she described.
Until their very souls leaped out,
Bleeding in nakedness before us,
Imbibed by her honesty,
And ready to shout;
Only obscured by the gulf
Between her consciousness and mine;
For traditional love guided my youth,
I saw her only as my mother.
As the safe haven whose ample skirts
Provided many a comforting fold,
In which I hid
From the multiple demons,
Of a child's domestic world.
I knew her as the ultimate power
Whose will and desire settled all disputes.
I knew her as the source of all wisdom
That enlightened me about human vagaries.
And she wished me to see her inner self,
The core she had become,
As life had groomed her,
Shaped and chiselled her,
Through strife since time began.
She knew the Eve
That was to Adam: a woman.
Said she:
"I am neither mother, wife, nor housewife.
I am Dorothy Sebastian."

BABY FATHER, BABY MOTHER

Baby Father,
Baby Mother,
Not home maker,
But society wrecker.
He held her,
Stroked her,
Kissed her,
Drained her dry
Of what dreams she had left.
She sucked him in,
Cradled him within
Her hungry sensuous loins;
Used him
To get a baby;
To get a flat,
She thought:
To get a life;
And that was that.
She had lost,
Her innocence,
At unknowing fourteen.
Hungry for love,
The caressing of care,
She'd opened her body,
Laid her soul bare
To a callous virgin taker.

He knew no other way,
To be a man;
But to make her,
Or any other like her,
To take her,
Abuse her.
Still with hope
She had tried,
To find love;
Twice or thrice or more;
It depended on
What she thought,
Of whom she told her score,
As he sexed her on life's floor.
Almost used up,
Though not yet eighteen,
Lost in life's quagmire,
Living on its edge,
She made a pledge:
She'd be the planner.
She invited him in;
Offered him,
Irresistible passion;
Showed him
What she had left;
Her body.
Like a hungry lioness
She devoured him.
It was easy;
She squeezed him within
Her ripened loins;

Drained him,
Used him,
To get a baby;
To get a flat,
And that was that.
She knew she had new life.
Baby fathers,
Baby mothers,
Not home makers,
Society wreckers.

YOUTH REVISITED

She saw him first; cool, the sort of dude
Her friends would get sweaty over.
He was revisiting his wasted life as a youth;
Saw her: the girl he could not get
At her age, in that stage,
When he was shy, clumsy and branded uncouth.
She saw a mirage of sophistication;
Because he was older and a worker.
Her eyes twinkled at the envy
On the faces of her friends,
As he drove her in life's fast lanes,
Swerving, screeching round the bends
Of its classy, moneyed streets.
He had not grown much
Beyond the stage she was at.
He appraised her rising well formed breasts,
And her broad flat thighs.
He saw white pearls
As her curved half open lips
Formed a small, yet inviting smile.
He felt them soft and yielding
As he kissed her,
In a world of day dreams,
Where everything was possible.

He moved closer and spoke:
Words, that with hope,
Would broaden her smile
And make it worthwhile
To spend time; his life with her.
She saw his lips open, moving and parted.
She heard his words spoken; her frown started
As his voice, broke the silence of her reverie.
She knew from this only real link between them,
That the falseness in his words had broken
Her illusion, her fantasy vision.
She realised with horror,
That her friends would think her absurd
To even smile with him,
This guy who was not cool,
And certainly no dude.
His words hung in unwanted space.
He saw her leave with quickening pace;
And knew that he had revisited his youth,
In that stage, when he was clumsy and uncouth.

PROTOCOL

How do you do?
How do you do?
An English greeting,
Exchanged at meeting.

How do you do?
How do you do?
It's just something
That we say.
That's the custom,
Like we pray,
Dressed at church,
On a Sunday.

How do you do?
How do you do?
Is the answer;
Does it matter?
Just friendly chatter.

How do you do?
How do you do
Favours secrecy
And diplomacy,
Leaves us strangers,
Friendship stranglers;
Frowns on intimacy,
Helps hypocrisy.

For if I did reply,
Told you how,
Told you why,
Do I care?
Do you care?
When I answer
Would you hear?
If I'm ill,
Or if I'm well,
Does it matter
If I tell?

How do you do?
How do you do?
Tried and tested,
So it's lasted.
It's the expected
Thing we say.
That's the custom,
Like we pray,
In church,
Dressed up
On a Sunday.

THE SALE IS ON

Competitive Consumption!
The sale is on!
Come to the sale!
Predictable no more,
It's after or before,
Stamped boldly on the door,
What ever grand season,
Quoted as the reason,
To intrude in our lives.
So that husbands and wives
Can regain their lost spark,
And again have a lark:
Gifts for consolation
To make restitution
For broken vows.

The sale is on!
Come to the sale!
In thousands we hustle.
We joggle, we bustle.
We run helter-skelter.
We don't stop to shelter.
Like cattle we jostle;
Stampeding we battle,
To get in. We struggle,
We hassle, we haggle,
The thinner and fatter
Together we barter.

For what do we cackle?
To be first in the queue,
To be ahead of you,
To be able to buy
That prize TV I spy,
For the price of the hat,
For the cheap cricket bat;
For the blue curtain set
For my new maisonette;
For the dining room suite,
For new shoes for my feet,
For the goods we don't need,
Yet we buy them through greed,
To show to my neighbour,
That for all his hard labour,
He'll never be better than me.

TOOTH PASTE AD

She saw him first
He saw her next.
She thought
and hid it,
'My irresistible man!
Aren't I lucky?
I'm here alone
in his space.
I'll make him play,
start the game
and I'll lose.
He'll win a date
To take me for a spin'
She smiled coyly,
with innocent shyness.
He responded coarsely;
mouth opened wide
as he spoke.
She saw his teeth, like black warts
in forbidden space.
She turned and left; with quickening pace.

THE ELECTRONIC BOSS

You struggle awake to the alarm beeper.
Wake up! Arise you lazy sleeper.
Get to work, for you've sold your time
To the universal electronic chime.

We work to the tune of the electronic boss.
She runs never ending, she doesn't care a toss.
She's above human laws and doesn't give us slack,
Because she's scientific, she is precisely exact.

You're driving along and you are told to stop;
Scared of a ticket, from an irate cop.
Ordered to a halt, by the droid traffic light.
You have sworn to obey the electronic knight.

"I'm the boss. I can't be wrong
I'm computerised and strong."

Getting to the work-place, you're ordered to clock in.
It's a figure of speech, you're just registering.
From your bed to your job, you cannot get away;
The electronic boss will determine your pay.

To get your pay cheque you consult Payroll,
It's all printed out on its electronic scroll,
If there is a blip, and you think it's all wrong,
The electronic boss just sings her swan song:

"I'm the boss. I can't be wrong;
I'm computerised and strong."

You relax in your home, looking at the T V.
You've eaten a meal and you're feeling sleepy.
You drowse and you drift, in the arms of your lover,
The whining phone disturbs you, the electronic
    trigger.

Your life's almost over, its driving force spent,
The doc plugs you into the electronic vent.
When its beep bleeps, a slow fading light,
You're dressed and laid out on life's final night.

The electronic boss has had the last say
And your cold feet of clay, get carted away.
"I'm the boss. I can't be wrong;
I'm computerised and strong."

THE JOURNEY

Dear youth,
Bankers of life,
Like driftwood
In its river,
Without strife,
Dragged as clay.
On ground-hog-day;
Repeating yesterday;
Living the future,
Like yester-year;
As some one drugged,
And without fear.

Who will you be?
In life's river,
In its span?
Do you
Have a plan?'
'I've no time
Life happens;
I'm too busy
Having fun:
I've got
Dice to shoot,
I've got
Life to loot!'

Caution youth!
Without a rudder,
You're drift-wood
In life's pool.
You start believing,
That you're drinking
Its elixir; cool.
But they're toxins,
That destroy
Your betrayed soul;
Waterlogged,
Full of stench,
You stagnate
In her trench;
Poisoned!

Enter rudderless
In its mainstream,
You get dragged
To her wide oceans.
Tossed by her demons;
Hungry for lost souls
Of those adrift;

Survival demands vigilance.
Its howling winds and angry waves
Roaring from its fathomless depths,
Demand your best.
If unprepared
Too late;
You lose control.

You pay the price
For undervalued life:
Death! Premature,
Untimely Death!

ON THE BANK OF THE RIVER OF LIFE

I'm standing on the bank of the river of life,
Looking to the future, but seeing only strife:
Strife in the family, between husband and wife;
Strife in the community, where anger is rife;
Strife on the streets, on the edge of a knife;
Strife in politics, it's not played with a fife;

Strife in the church, precepts are corrupted;
Strife in the nation, where power is corroded;
Strife in world society, whose leaders can't be
    counted;
Strife in human species, over skins that are
    pigmented;
Strife in the sharing, the poor are neglected;
Strife in the U. N, where corruption is detected.

I'm standing on the bank of the river of life.
Looking to the future and seeing strife is rife.
When I was a child I was carefree, happy.
I larked like a bird, I played in my nappy,
Now I am a man, I am worn out with care,
Living each day with a background of fear:

Fearing my child may not live to see twenty,
Fearing my world may one day be as empty
As a black hole in the void of outer space,
And like the species we destroyed, our race
May become lost; wiped out without trace.

I was standing on the bank of the river of life,
I entered its stream but was stranded by strife,
Was I a pilot of such poor degree?
Are all mankind of the same pedigree?

We've entered the stream of the river of life,
We've polluted, and plundered; destruction is rife.
We look for a saviour; we should look to ourselves;
Shake complacency from the impotent shelves.

We must swim together in the river of life,
With hope in our hands, we must conquer strife
For the birth of a future: a retrieved paradise.

INSEPARABLE PARTNERS

How can I move on?
I am stuck in the quagmire of despair.
Death crept in and took the light of my life.
It cares not whether it is beloved husband or wife,
Or father, mother, brother sister, or friend;
Its relentless trail moves unnoticed to the prey;
Then folds its dark mantle and takes the life away,
Leaving the living, mourning and crying, fearing the
    dying.

In my grief,
I take not pleasure in the thought of hope:
That death is friend to life;
That death makes way, for new life to sway;
That in the passing of my light
New birth took flight;
That one was born, as mine was lost,
I only mourn, weep and count the cost
Of my jewel stolen, forever gone.

I rage and shout my curses to the skies.
With haggard brows, and frowns and bloodshot eyes,
Deep in their sockets, red, devoid of sleep,
I mourn continuous and in public weep.
That death, its toll has robbed me of my prize;.
And I, now rudderless at sea,
Am lost for all eternity.

But look within your self and ask:
'For whom do I weep?'
Is it for your lost love, your dear departed,
Taken forever, when you never had consented?
Can that be, when we know that life and death
Are twins, separated only by a breath?

'For whom do I weep?'
It could be for your own mortality;
For the passing of the living into finality,
Especially of one so close as a beloved,
Brings the gaping hungry grave, shrouded
With no buffer; and slipping on life's floor,
You fear that next, death may drag you through its
       door.

THE MUSIC THERAPIST

The music therapist enters
The world of thriving disharmony:
The world of those whose lives
Are shattered beyond repair,
Lost in the maelstrom of despair.

He offers:
From unfathomed corners of his being,
The magic keys of harmony,
Which spring like threads from the strings
Of music in their souls,
To soothe their undying pain,
That like a storm pours
Down like showers in relentless rain.

He offers:
Empathy, therapy,
A face of love
To lost spirits;
Young ones and old souls,
Befuddled, bedraggled,
Like beggars of earth,
Painfully scanning
The void of their lives,
Hungering for comfort,
For understanding,
For satisfying meaning,
In a life almost over;

Searching desperately
For a safe haven:
A peaceful space,
In each torrid frightened mind.

The music therapist enters this world,
And from his source of music played
And music to be made,
He lights a spark
Of no measurable size,
In the creative soul
That we all possess;
And opens up a path
Of true redemption,
That each tortured patient,
Can follow
To a space of peace,
Where life and death,
And all the in-between,
Can be laid to rest.

I GRIEVED MY BROTHER'S DEATH

I grieved my brother's death,

And walked in morbid daze,

Around the streets of life,

Within myself in strife;

To find the hidden reason

That would explain the maze

Of pathways taken, that led

In his bloom, to death.

The pain I felt lay deep,

In the chasms of my soul;

For he was life portrayed,

In the best of me arrayed.

I DANCED ON THE BEACH

I danced on the beach where the fishermen walked
Who gave me bold stares, as their steps I stalked,
Through straits, rough troughs and billows white,
They had trapped their catch in the dawning light.

I danced on the beach where their harvest was shared;
Fruits of their blood, sweat, and joy for lives spared.
They had worked for the day and had gone home to
    play;
Now the beach was mine, and I danced away.

I danced on the beach with the wind in my face.
I was naked to nature, moved freely in space,
With boldness and daring to the music of my heart
I danced like a dervish, at the whirlwind's start.

I danced on the beach, nude in my beauty
Virgin awakening, bold in anxiety,
Thrilled by this freedom and a strange compulsion,
To be daring, bold, to dance with passion.

I danced on the beach; there was joy in my freedom
To be wantonly naked, flaunt society's wisdom,
In tune with sun, sky, earth and the sea
Was my first true fulfilment, my sheer ecstasy.

SINGLE MOTHER

She touched the crumpled bed sheets
as gently as her kisses
had caressed his lips,
on those hot nights,
of endless passionate bliss.
Her smile began,
changed into a grin,
and cackled into a crescendo of screams.
He was no longer there
to envelop her,
to lick the pain and grime of life away.
He had met her
with dreams and yearning,
had offered exquisite soothing,
quenching her longing.
Then he had gone!
leaving her
unfulfilled and bleeding.

She lay on the bed,
As she'd done for him;
felt his hot hands
on her yielding flesh,
like volcanic spasms
searing her mind,
filling her body
leaving her blind
to reality:

blind to the vandalism of the world
outside the sanctuary of their bed.
For in that space
was her still universe,
where peace filled her being,
and hateful passions fled.
A voice calls out,
seeking help,
speaks her name,
sneaking into her reverie,
shattering her calm
like broken glass,
reminding her of her pain.
She answers their child,
the fruit of love shared.
Leaving the sanctuary of their bed,
she rejoins the world..
lifting her son
with her haunting lover's face implanted.
He smiles with seductive eyes,
twinkling, searing her heart.
Her embrace tightens,
her frame relaxes with a start:
Her lover has gone,
but the best of him
will never depart.

A WOMAN FALSE

Oh wicked witch when first we met
We loved, I thought, without regret.
Why did you hide your natural face?
Behind your screen of mocking lace?
Blinkered I was to see you fair,
With beauty thin, a false veneer;
Your soulless eyes were just a stare,
Like Arctic waste, so cold and bare.
You carved an abyss in my life
That you set out to fill with strife.
While I in blissful ignorance,
Gave all I had; caught in your trance.
Your acts of loving, were not for me.
Strangers thought: how lovely, he's lucky.
She loves him much, it's plain to see.
Feigned love was wicked mockery.

Could I but see behind your mask,
The one portrayed, I thought you were;
No wasted years I'd spend before,
I found my true, dear love.

LADY IN THE PICTURE

She sits and stares with radiant smile.
She changes not with time,
This portrait of a young woman
On love's threshold
Meets the model,
Now feeble and old,
Smiling back.

What memories pass between them?
The old woman hugs herself
In remembrance of past loves,
Past kisses and a life
That can never return.
She smiles at her painting,
Reassured that yes, it was real.
It did happen in her past life;
She had been beautiful.

From behind, he gently pivots her.
She sees another portrait in his eyes;
Eyes that bathe her with his love,
That always transported her above
Life's mundane mediocrity;
To their place of happy tranquility.
'You are beautiful and I love you.'
And she knew that she was loved.

LITTLE BABE

Little babe, little babe, how will you fare,
Born in a world full of hate and despair?
If you could speak, what would you say?
Be grateful for life; be hopeful each day?

You see not the time-bombs, we've laid in your path,
You know not: the arctic is melting up north,
That the cosmos around, earth's cocoon of life,
We're killing by greed, destroying by strife.

Little babe, little babe, it's almost too late
To save your world, from our destructive fate,
We've started the process; we'll give it to you
Contrite with hope, that you'll see it through.

NOSTALGIA

I listened as the piano played that tune;
music shared with my father and mother,
played in my youth, by my sister and brother.
I was wafted back to days of happy innocence,
when, no burdens blighted my life;
then, family love enveloped us like warm safe
blankets.
The haunting melody wrapped its folds around my
    heart.
Gently my tears flowed as I saw my parents,
ghosts of spent life, smiling with love,
bright as stars on a sunny evening,
shining in their eyes, lighting up my dreams.
If only I had known that those were my happiest
    days.
I wished; I wished in vain...
for the return of past youthful innocence.
I'd been too young to know.

The music flowed;
bringing scents and pictures of my past,
dragging the sadness of nostalgia
Like lazy, hazy mists I could not touch or shape.
For now I live the life of barren dreams:
where promises are meant to be broken,
like a house of glass on a seismic fault;
where honour is subservient to expediency,
where innocence is born to be abused.

I wished; I wished in vain
for those happy alpha days,
when music, shared with my father and mother,
was played in my youth, by my sister and brother.

But hope rose in my heart,
when I looked and saw the child of my loins,
playing the music that I first had heard
in my youth:
music shared with my father and mother;
music played by my sister and brother.

TO SWEET PAT, WITH LOVE

In life's train each day they sat,
'Cross the aisle from Dean was Pat,
Each to work the daily grind,
Not the plan God had in mind.

Seeds she planted in his heart
Trust to grow and love to start;
And they blossomed and they flourished
Then they swore they'd never part.

Pat the bride thereafter said
When their vows together read:
'I will love him 'till I'm dead,
For his heart will be my bed.'

Dean has loved her since they met;
Love devoted, in stone set.
She was every thing he wanted
Love so strong was holy planted.

And there-after Pat and Dean
Loving pair we all have seen;
Happiness to both was dear,
Pat's sweet food you too could share.

Sweet she was and like a rose,
Smile that pierced through any pose,
Eyes that sparkled friendly greeting,
Warmed your heart, with every meeting.

Every one was dear to her;
Christian love she would offer.
Any one in need of care
Sweet Pat's charity would bear.

She was mindful of her work,
For her church she'd never shirk,
Duty, promises she'd keep.
And for sinners she would weep.

If you wish to find dear Pat,
Go up high and in the crowd
Of God's good souls, she'd be sat,
Speaking of her love so proud:

Of grand children and her daughter,
Of her husband and their laughter,
Through a life of happiness,
That was her creative bliss.

So rest in peace sweet spirit gone,
For your life has just begun
In the arms of our greatest love,
Jesus Christ, sacrificial dove.

With love to Dean, Sandra, and Family

FIRST LOVE

I first saw Francesca caught in the rain,
The sun saw her too and came out again.
The clouds thought her pretty and changed their hue
I fell deeply and knew the love was true.

Her walk was so rhythmic, a natural dance,
Her smile hypnotic, held me entranced.
Enraptured by her beauty, her kindly eyes,
I told her I loved her and claimed the prize.

She told me she loved me; what a surprise!
I promised love forever, without any lies.
She told me that to seal it, we'd have to kiss.
Of course I did not falter, that kiss was bliss.

Francesca told Loraine, her girlfriend next door,
Loraine came to me, for proof to be sure.
She asked me to kiss her, so she could believe.
I gave her what was sacred, I was so naïve.

Francesca passed me coldly, we never spoke again,
I could not understand it; my love, it did not wane.
My friends gave me distractions and soon I did forget
Francesca, Loraine, all girls: I was only eight.

LOVE BY PROXY

We sat behind the garden hedge
And ogled Wendy Turner,
She danced among the dainty veg,
Oh boy! She was a stunner.

He sent me as his messenger,
My clever older brother.
Tell her that I love her
And give her my love letter.

I did. Said I: 'He loves you,
But I love you too.'
'Hey kid! Say that again.'
I echoed the refrain.

She asked in a voice of quiet calm
'What do you know of love?'
'Your eyes are warm,
Your lips well curved;
Your smile lights up the sky.
You're prettier than the Queen. So say I'

She laughed,
Soft sexy sounds that made me swell,
And filled my heart with hope.
'Tell him,' she said, 'take a spell.
Jump the moon, lick a spoon.

I cannot kiss a dope.
Your words are sweet,
You deserve a treat.
Come then, sit here'
Up close I went
With great intent, but yet a little nervous;
'Now no more words; your actions vent;
Let's see, can you be amorous?'
I held her close, locked lips craved more
My warm life juices flowed.
Our frenzied actions to explore
Were wild, audacious, bold.
But as we raved in love so racy,
With fevered ecstasy,
I felt a hand; my mother spoke:
'School-time! Wake up!
And I awoke.'

THE PROPOSAL

Eight-year Marion Steinbeck,
Sat on my knee,
Arms around my neck,
She kisses me.
'I have a secret for you,'
She whispers in my ear.

'Gary and I will marry
Before the end of year.'
'Congratulations darling,
Wonderful my pet!
When did he propose?'
'I have not told him yet.'

THE ARTIST AND THE CHILD

A child saw an artist at work one day.
'What are you doing?'
The child asked in play.
'I am doing my art,'
The artist replied.
And what is your art?
Curiosity cried.
'To paint something beautiful,'
The artist tried.
'Oh!' said the child,
'So you are the person who paints
All the pretty flowers and lovely butterflies.
Do you paint rainbows too?'

REVERIE IN SPACE

What do you know of your lover,
beautifully curved,
sitting beside you?
You can touch her and be thrilled,
but do you know her
as she sits, lost in mysterious reverie;
gone somewhere perhaps to be free,
sitting there beside you, in your space,
with an enigmatic smile on her face?

Can it be that she is lost
in the space of another,
although you can reach
and be thrilled as you touch her?.

Where is the woman, your lover?
You know her name.
Where has she gone?
Call her, she looks just the same,
as the happy carefree person you first met.
Was it pain or sweet happiness,
that drove her on
to vacant space
in her eyes and in her smile?

One thing you know, she is real;
sensuously curved next to you,
you can reach over
and touch her and be thrilled.

Like the world,
you can claim it and her;
but what do you know of your lover,
in the deep space where she has gone,
lost in its vastness without trace,
sitting there beside you, in your space?

Yet you can reach over
And touch her and be thrilled.

FLYING HIGH

I took my lover to the moon,
She held me close, but did not swoon.
We travelled on the wings of love
Soaring higher, the stars above
Lit up our path, as swift we flew
And swifter still, our passions grew,
Through time and space, and kiss by kiss,
We entered paradise.

I took my lover to the moon
But not in Sputnik, or balloon.
I took her on the wings of trust
Away from barriers, that rust
Love's wheels of freedom to express
Itself; its whims; that see excess
In love's imaginings. We flew
On Cupid's wings of hope and grew
Close bonds of love that, forever won
Our hearts and made us live as one.

I took my lover to the moon,
Assured her that our star was set,
And resting, sighing on my breast
Upon its cusp, we cast our nest.
We cast it for the rest of time
And kiss by kiss,
We stayed in paradise.

BEVERLEY AND BILL

Four centuries long it seemed,
Though four years only,
You stirred a fire within me
That only your love could quench.
When you kissed with such tenderness,
When you crushed me to your breast,
And held me to your heart beat
I knew you loved me.
And when each day you held me close,
I knew you loved me and did not ask.
I thought you shy, did not espy
Another reason why,
The man I loved and loved me back,
Had never said he did.
I was too bubbly like a kid,
Too happy, and on the cloud of love
I lay, a gift at your feet.

Like a toy to add to your collection,
You tore at the wrapping,
And I lay bare: your ripened fruit,
In passion taken, yet vulnerable.
Was I just a pretty little fluff,
Or was I goddess of your heart
As you were, god to me?

Four centuries long,
I suspended hung
Eating, drinking hope,
Until hope became reality in my dream;
Although you said not: 'I love you.'

Four sweet centuries, infinity of joy
When you were love:
The blazing sun and amber sky,
The rainy day with dimpled sea,
The singing wind, the rippling river,
The honeyed garden, continuous fever,
When everything was love.
But then you spoke.
You bared your soul.
Was there a need?
You told truth, tenderly,
In solemn painful tones,
Said: 'I have been playing with a toy,
Four centuries long,
But now at last I love you.'
And then I left.
I fled to find my soul again.

LOVE FOREVER LOST

I speak to you who love.
You are loved and blessed with the care of another.
Some one so special, that your every waking moment
Is primed, consumed with thoughts of your lover;
For your sense of that love
Lies just below the surface of your world.

You live each minute anchored in your being,
Strong because of the lover you are seeing:
Someone special loves you.
That you are precious to some one else, is the thought
That burns in your heart and sets your world alight.
You glow in the radiance of your love.
Friends see the light and ask: who is your dove?
You smile at first, coy in your secret;
But it reaches out primed like electricity,
Until you burst with the force of your passion.
'Let the world know that this fruit of our union;
Must be shared with everyone,
Lest we explode with love's intensity.'
So you share the knowledge of your love.
You bask in its greatness and uniqueness:
'No others have ever loved like us before.
Ours is the most incredible of loves.'
You are known as the two in one.
There go the lovers, inseparable.
Others marvel at your iconic status.

But dark furies rear their heads: you must be careful
Lest the special essence of your love is coveted.
From this unique strength a question sneaks into your
　　mind:
Can it be stolen from beneath the pedestal our love
　　refined?
The intruding unease is brushed aside
But still persists, to tarnish
What had been so grand and without blemish.

Must we go veiled to keep secure the love so vital to
　　our happiness?
Must we in secret love, to hide from predators our
　　treasure?

The answer lies in honesty and selflessness of loving,
In your need less to receive; more in your generosity
　　of giving,
In savouring and nurturing the person who is your
　　lover,
As you met; not trying to change your love into
　　another.
Embracing that morning star that lit your heart
And made the atoms of your world
Race to the extremities of the universe
For in the first doubting of that love,
You risk your lover will slip away,
Crushed by the uncertainty you display
And will not stay.

Love forever lost; lost love; the sadness of our lives;
For what happiness can be greater
Than the certainty of being loved;
Of living an eternity with your lover?

REMINISCING

There's none so sad as waking up to know what you
have lost:

Her smile, her warmth, her wistful look, the happy
past;

Her gentle touch, her thoughtfulness, the laughter
you both shared;

Her love, its passion, tenderness, the joys you dared.

Yours was a love so rare, to be treasured with great
care,

What madness made you drive her out, and leave you
in despair?

Did she not soothe your tortured soul and kiss your
frowns away?

Did she not give you all she had; your foul nights
turned to day?

To you her love was limitless and thus was freedom
born,

For in the safety of its nest, no more were you forlorn.

She knew you well, could instant tell, how flew the
    breeze your way;

Thoughts were enough for her to hear, the words
    your heart would say.

She asked for nought, except your love; and this she
    would not measure;

It was enough you were her love; your life, it was her
    treasure.

With wistful eyes she gazed at you, in loving
    tenderness,

You were her world, she felt complete, in total
    happiness.

Why must we lose the ones we need, before we count
    the cost?

Why do we clasp so close what kills; destroys us
    most?

What's left is hope, with love that's deep, you can but
    pray and offer:
All that you were, can be again, and next chance do
not falter.

WINTER

Outside,
The wintry God,
Bombards with icy bolts,
The warmth my love,
Like summer's rays
Had embalmed my soul with storing.
I care not:
How frost and icy shafts,
Cover the paths
That I must tread;
The furnace of your love,
Keeps me warm.

I feel the heat of your touch,
Here, there, everywhere.
My thoughts,
Like red hot bolts of lightening,
Remembering your kisses,
Your words of hungry passion,
Melt the winter's onslaught;
And shrouds me,
In a cocoon of love.

Snug in bed,
With your yielding body,
Wrapped around me,
Contentedly,
I smile and kiss the life,
Your lips,
Like honeyed nectar, offer.
I love you.

LIFE'S LIKE THAT

Always remember
Down rapid,
O'er fall,
That life's like that;
After all.
Beyond every rapid,
Glides a stream;
Below every fall,
A glistening pool,
Of life's cool,
Wholesome elixir.
 It will seem,
That life's like that,
After all:
A perilous time
Down rapid,
O'er fall;
Then peace;
And your life's a sweet dream.

ABOUT THE AUTHOR

John Prince was born, during a hurricane, in the Caribbean island of Nevis. He was schooled in the Leeward Islands and graduated from the Government Teachers' College in Port of Spain, Trinidad, after which, he did some teaching in Antigua. In 1957 he emigrated to the UK, where he worked as a teacher in North and East London. He eventually became an ILEA Head Teacher of Homerton House Boys Comprehensive School in Hackney, East London.

He was further educated at London University, at the Institute of Education, where he gained an M.A. (Econ. of Ed.).

In March 2007, on the occasion of the Bicentenary Celebrations of the Abolition of the Trans-Atlantic Slave Trade, the Hackney Museum, London, acquired two of his poems for their archives.